ALONE LIFE AT OLD AGE SOLUTION BOOK

"Alone but Not Lonely: Solutions for a Happy and Healthy Old Age"

BLESS P. ALLWELL

TABLE OF CONTENTS

CHAPTER 1

"NAVIGATING SOLITUDE WITH PURPOSE"

As individuals transition into the later stages of life, navigating the path of solitude can be a daunting prospect. However, "Alone but Not Lonely" begins its journey by encouraging readers to embrace this solo phase with a sense of purpose and optimism. This chapter lays the foundation for a fulfilling exploration of old age, highlighting the opportunities that arise when one learns to navigate solitude with intention.

1.1 Embracing the Solo Journey

Embracing the solo journey is not about resigning oneself to isolation; it's about recognizing the unique opportunities for self-discovery and growth that come with solitude. The first section of this chapter delves into the mindset shift required to view this stage of life not as an ending but as a new beginning. Embracing the solo journey is about acknowledging that life continues to unfold, presenting fresh possibilities for learning, adventure, and personal fulfillment.

In exploring this theme, the chapter addresses the societal stigma often attached to aging alone. It challenges stereotypes and encourages readers to view solitude not as a limitation but as a canvas upon which one can paint a rich and vibrant tapestry of experiences. Embracing the solo journey involves cultivating a positive mindset, allowing individuals to savor the freedom and flexibility that come with this stage of life.

1.2 Crafting a Meaningful Life Story

Central to navigating solitude with purpose is the concept of crafting a meaningful life story. In this section, the chapter delves into the importance of reflection and intentionality in shaping one's narrative. Whether through journaling, memoir writing, or engaging in conversations with loved ones, the process of crafting a meaningful life story empowers individuals to recognize the value and impact of their experiences.

The chapter explores various tools and exercises that aid in this reflective process. From recounting pivotal life moments to identifying core values and passions, readers are guided through a journey of self-discovery. Crafting a meaningful life story is not just a therapeutic exercise; it serves as a roadmap for the future, helping individuals set intentions and goals for their solo years based on a deep understanding of who they are and what they value.

1.3 Strategies for Finding Purpose in Solitude

As the chapter progresses, it transitions to practical strategies for finding purpose in solitude. It recognizes that purpose is the fuel that propels individuals forward, giving meaning to each day. This section provides a toolkit of strategies tailored to the unique circumstances of navigating old age alone.

The exploration begins with the importance of setting realistic and achievable goals. From small daily accomplishments to more significant milestones, each achievement becomes a building block in the construction of a purpose-driven life. The chapter also emphasizes the significance of staying engaged with lifelong passions and interests, encouraging readers to explore new hobbies or revisit activities that once brought them joy.

Finding purpose in solitude extends beyond individual fulfillment; it often involves contributing to the well-being of others. Volunteering, mentoring, or participating in community projects are avenues explored in this section. The sense of purpose derived from making a positive impact on others not only enhances one's own well-being but also fosters a sense of interconnectedness with the broader community.

In essence, Chapter 1 lays the groundwork for a transformative journey into the later years of life. It challenges the notion that solitude is synonymous with loneliness and offers readers the tools and mindset shifts needed to navigate this phase with purpose, optimism, and a commitment to personal growth. "Alone but Not Lonely" encourages individuals to see their solo journey as an opportunity for reinvention, self-discovery, and the cultivation of a deeply meaningful life.

CHAPTER 2
"THRIVING IN INDEPENDENCE"

Navigating the journey of aging alone involves more than just an emotional mindset—it requires practical strategies to ensure a secure, comfortable, and fulfilling solo future. In this chapter, "Alone but Not Lonely" explores key aspects of thriving in independence, ranging from financial planning to creating a safe living space and managing healthcare and wellness with autonomy.

2.1 Financial Planning for a Solo Future

The first pillar of thriving in independence centers around financial planning—an essential aspect of securing a stable and worry-free solo future. This section of the chapter begins by addressing the unique financial considerations that come with aging alone. It encourages readers to take stock of their current financial situation, evaluate potential expenses in the years to come, and explore ways to optimize their financial health.

Discussions on budgeting, retirement savings, and investments are tailored to the specific needs of those navigating old age solo. The chapter emphasizes the importance of creating a realistic and sustainable financial plan, considering potential healthcare costs, housing expenses, and leisure activities. Additionally, it explores avenues for supplementing income, such as part-time work, freelance opportunities, or pursuing passions that can also generate income.

Financial literacy is presented as a tool for empowerment, allowing individuals to make informed decisions about their money. The chapter guides readers through resources and strategies for enhancing their financial knowledge, from consulting with financial advisors to utilizing online tools and educational programs.

2.2 Creating a Comfortable and Safe Living Space

The second component of thriving in independence revolves around creating a living space that is both comfortable and safe. This section recognizes that the home environment plays a crucial role in overall well-being and independence, especially for those navigating the later years of life alone.

The chapter provides practical advice on assessing and adapting living spaces to meet changing needs. It covers topics such as home modifications for increased accessibility, optimizing lighting and layout for safety, and incorporating technology to enhance security.

Whether readers choose to age in place or explore alternative housing options, the emphasis is on creating a living space that aligns with individual preferences and fosters a sense of independence.

Beyond physical adaptations, the chapter also delves into the emotional and social dimensions of the living environment. It explores strategies for cultivating a positive and nurturing home atmosphere, including the benefits of incorporating hobbies, meaningful decor, and elements that spark joy and connection. The goal is to empower individuals to take control of their living space, ensuring it becomes a sanctuary that enhances their overall quality of life.

2.3 Navigating Healthcare and Wellness Alone

The third and equally critical aspect of thriving in independence involves navigating healthcare and wellness without the traditional support systems of a family or partner. This section acknowledges the challenges that can arise in managing health independently and provides a comprehensive guide to proactive and preventive healthcare.

The chapter explores strategies for building a robust healthcare support network, including the selection of healthcare providers, specialists, and the development of a reliable emergency plan. It discusses the importance of regular health check-ups, screenings, and fostering open communication with healthcare professionals.

Preventive wellness becomes a central theme, covering topics such as nutrition, exercise, mental health, and social engagement. The chapter emphasizes the role of self-care in maintaining overall well-being and preventing potential health issues. It encourages readers to explore activities and practices that contribute to physical, emotional, and mental health, tailoring recommendations to individual preferences and abilities.

Additionally, the chapter addresses the importance of advanced care planning, ensuring that individuals have a voice in their healthcare decisions even when they may not have immediate family members. It covers the creation of living wills, healthcare proxies, and other legal documents that reflect personal preferences for end-of-life care.

In essence, Chapter 2 of "Alone but Not Lonely" equips individuals with the tools and knowledge to navigate the practical aspects of aging alone. By addressing financial planning, creating a safe and comfortable living space, and managing healthcare and wellness independently, this chapter empowers readers to not only thrive but also find fulfillment in their solo journey through the later years of life.

CHAPTER 3

"BUILDING A SUPPORTIVE NETWORK"

While navigating the later years of life alone, building and maintaining a supportive network becomes paramount for emotional well-being, companionship, and a sense of belonging. Chapter 3 of "Alone but Not Lonely" explores various dimensions of creating a robust support system, from fostering relationships with loved ones to leveraging technology and joining communities tailored for solo seniors.

3.1 Fostering Relationships with Loved Ones

The foundation of a supportive network often begins with fostering and strengthening existing relationships with loved ones. This section of the chapter acknowledges the significance of family, friends, and social connections in enhancing the quality of life for those navigating old age alone.

The chapter encourages readers to initiate and maintain open communication with family members and close friends, sharing their thoughts, feelings, and concerns. It explores strategies for staying connected, even if geographically distant, through regular phone calls, video chats, and visits when possible. Additionally, it delves into the importance of building a reliable and trustworthy circle of individuals who can offer support during times of need.

For those who may not have immediate family, the chapter explores avenues for creating chosen families—relationships formed with friends, neighbors, or community members who provide companionship, emotional support, and assistance when required. It emphasizes the value of reciprocal relationships, where individuals contribute to the well-being of others as well.

3.2 Connecting in a Digital Age: Technology and Social Media

In an era dominated by technology, this section of the chapter explores the role of digital tools and social media in connecting with others. Recognizing that technology can bridge geographical gaps and facilitate communication, "Alone but Not Lonely" guides readers through the potential benefits of incorporating technology into their social lives.

The chapter covers topics such as setting up and navigating social media accounts, participating in online forums and discussion groups, and utilizing video conferencing platforms to stay connected with friends and family. It emphasizes the importance of digital literacy, offering guidance on overcoming potential barriers and fears associated with technology use.

Exploring the digital landscape also opens avenues for discovering shared interests, joining online communities, and accessing resources tailored to specific needs and preferences. The chapter highlights the potential of technology to expand social circles, providing avenues for meeting new people, engaging in virtual activities, and staying informed about community events.

3.3 Joining Communities and Clubs for Solo Seniors

Recognizing the power of shared experiences, this section of the chapter explores the benefits of joining communities and clubs specifically designed for solo seniors. It acknowledges that purposeful engagement with like-minded individuals can foster a sense of belonging, reduce feelings of isolation, and create opportunities for socialization and mutual support.

The chapter introduces various types of communities, from local senior centers and clubs to online forums and meetup groups. It provides guidance on finding communities aligned with individual interests, whether they revolve around hobbies, cultural activities, or wellness initiatives. Joining these groups not only offers social interaction but also opens doors to potential friendships and a shared sense of purpose.

For those who may face physical limitations or prefer remote interactions, the chapter explores virtual communities and clubs that cater to a wide range of interests. It discusses the potential of book clubs, hobby groups, and support networks that operate in an online space, fostering connections and friendships irrespective of physical proximity.

In essence, Chapter 3 of "Alone but Not Lonely" serves as a comprehensive guide to building a supportive network that enriches the lives of those navigating the later years alone. By fostering relationships with loved ones, embracing technology and social media, and actively participating in communities and clubs tailored for solo seniors, individuals are empowered to create a robust support system that enhances their overall well-being and contributes to a fulfilling solo journey.

CHAPTER 4

"HOLISTIC WELL-BEING IN THE GOLDEN YEARS"

As individuals navigate the golden years alone, prioritizing holistic well-being becomes instrumental in fostering a fulfilling and purposeful life. Chapter 4 of "Alone but Not Lonely" delves into the intricacies of well-rounded health—addressing physical fitness, mental wellness, and spiritual fulfillment. This comprehensive approach aims to empower readers to embrace the later years with vitality and tranquility.

4.1 Embracing Physical Health: Exercise and Nutrition

The foundation of well-being lies in physical health, and this section of the chapter begins with a deep dive into the importance of embracing exercise and maintaining a balanced nutritional lifestyle. Recognizing that physical health is not only crucial for longevity but also impacts mental and emotional well-being, "Alone but Not Lonely" provides practical insights tailored for those navigating the later years solo.

The chapter introduces a spectrum of exercises suitable for various fitness levels and physical abilities. From low-impact activities like walking and yoga to strength training and flexibility exercises, it emphasizes the importance of finding an approach that aligns with individual preferences and health conditions. The goal is to promote an active lifestyle that enhances mobility, prevents chronic conditions, and contributes to an overall sense of vitality.

Complementary to physical activity is a discussion on nutrition, exploring balanced and nourishing dietary choices. The chapter provides guidance on creating meal plans that address specific nutritional needs for seniors, including considerations for bone health, heart health, and maintaining a healthy weight.

It encourages readers to view nutrition as a tool for sustaining energy levels, promoting cognitive function, and supporting overall physical well-being.

4.2 Cultivating Mental Wellness: Cognitive Activities and Mindfulness

The journey to holistic well-being extends to mental wellness, acknowledging the interconnectedness of the mind and body. In this section, "Alone but Not Lonely" explores strategies for cultivating cognitive activities and mindfulness practices that contribute to mental acuity, emotional balance, and a resilient mindset.

The chapter introduces a range of cognitive activities designed to stimulate the brain and promote mental agility. From puzzles and games to lifelong learning pursuits, it encourages readers to engage in activities that challenge the mind, fostering creativity and cognitive resilience. The goal is to celebrate the ongoing capacity for learning and intellectual growth in the later years.

Mindfulness practices become a central theme, with the chapter providing practical guidance on incorporating meditation, deep breathing exercises, and mindfulness techniques into daily life. Recognizing the potential benefits of mindfulness for stress reduction, emotional well-being, and improved sleep, the chapter emphasizes the role of these practices in enhancing overall mental health.

Moreover, the section explores the connection between mental wellness and social engagement, encouraging readers to prioritize meaningful interactions, engage in conversations, and build relationships that contribute positively to their emotional health. It reinforces the idea that mental wellness is not only an individual endeavor but is enriched through connections with others.

4.3 Spiritual Fulfillment: Finding Tranquility in Solitude

Completing the trifecta of holistic well-being is the exploration of spiritual fulfillment. This section recognizes that spirituality is a deeply personal and individual aspect of well-being, often intertwined with a sense of purpose, connection, and inner tranquility.

The chapter encourages readers to explore and define their own spiritual beliefs and practices, whether they align with a religious tradition, philosophical principles, or a more secular understanding of spirituality. It highlights the potential for spiritual fulfillment to provide a source of strength, resilience, and a deeper connection to life's meaning and purpose.

For some, finding spiritual fulfillment may involve engaging in meditation, prayer, or contemplative practices. The chapter explores the benefits of these activities in promoting a sense of tranquility and inner peace, especially in the solitude of the later years. It emphasizes the potential for spiritual practices to be a source of comfort, solace, and a pathway to connecting with something greater than oneself.

In essence, Chapter 4 of "Alone but Not Lonely" serves as a guide to cultivating holistic well-being in the golden years. By embracing physical health through exercise and nutrition, fostering mental wellness through cognitive activities and mindfulness, and finding spiritual fulfillment in solitude, individuals navigating the later years alone are empowered to create a balanced and fulfilling lifestyle that contributes to their overall well-being and quality of life.